Drawing in Ash

WILL STONE, born 1966, is a poet, literary translator and essayist who divides his time between England and Belgium. His first collection of poetry, *Glaciation* (Salt, 2007), won the international Glen Dimplex Award for poetry in 2008. This is his second collection.

Will's published translations of poetry include *To The Silenced — Selected Poems of Georg Trakl* (Arc Publications, 2005). *Stefan Zweig — Journeys*, a first English translation of the celebrated Austrian writer's travel essays, was published in October 2010 by Hesperus Press. Translations of poetry by Belgian symbolist poets Emile Verhaeren and Georges Rodenbach are forthcoming from Arc in April 2011.

Also by Will Stone:

POETRY
Glaciation (Salt Publishing, 2007)

TRANSLATIONS
Les Chimères—Gérard de Nerval (Menard Press, 1999)
To The Silenced—Georg Trakl (Arc Publications, 2005)
Journeys—Stefan Zweig (Hesperus Press, 2010)
Selected Poems of Emile Verhaeren (Arc Publications, 2011)
Selected Poems of Georges Rodenbach (Arc Publications, 2011)

Drawing in Ash

WILL STONE

LONDON

PUBLISHED BY SALT PUBLISHING
Acre House, 11–15 William Road, London NW1 3ER, United Kingdom
All rights reserved

© Will Stone, 2011

The right of Will Stone to be identified as the
author of this work has been asserted by him in accordance
with Section 77 of the Copyright, Designs and Patents Act 1988.

This book is in copyright. Subject to statutory exception
and to provisions of relevant collective licensing agreements,
no reproduction of any part may take place without the written
permission of Salt Publishing.

Salt Publishing 2011

Printed and bound in Great Britain by
CPI Antony Rowe, Chippenham and Eastbourne

Typeset in Swift 9.5 / 13

This book is sold subject to the conditions that it shall not,
by way of trade or otherwise, be lent, re-sold, hired out,
or otherwise circulated without the publisher's prior consent
in any form of binding or cover other than that in which
it is published and without a similar condition including this
condition being imposed on the subsequent purchaser.

ISBN 978 1 84471 796 5 paperback

1 3 5 7 9 8 6 4 2

for Emma Mountcastle

Contents

I

Guided Tour Of The Ruins	5
The Extinction Plan	6
Christ On The Cross—Delacroix	8
Nietzsche At The End	10
Sometimes This Genius Grows Dark	11
Ice Warning	13
Walser's Last Walk	14
Secret Of The Picpus Cemetery, Paris	15
The Lonely Ones	17
Harrowing	18
The Clearing	19
Montaigne's Flight	21
Fatal Thrust	22
Loss Of Habitat	24
Condolence Packet	25
In A Lonely Place	26
Lenz	27
Checkpoint	28
I Am Charles Meryon	30
After Shingle Street	31
Chopin In Scotland	32
Horse Cure	34
Hawkridge	36
Young Lions With Their Kill	37
I Am The Reader	38
The Silence	40
In Culbone	41
In The Ancient Cemetery Of Ukkel	42
The Fears Of Charles Baudelaire	43
Darkness On Darkness	44

Fate of the Juvenile Gull	45
Repeat Offenders	46
The Antwerp Mannequins	48
Faces In An Orchestra	49
Advance Of A Rain Storm	50

II

Drawing In Ash	57
The Survivors	58
The Shriek	60
Spy Hole	61
Last Hours In The Flak Tower	63
Closer	65
The Clip	67
History Lesson	68
Dead Heading	69
Note Scribbled To The Unsaved	71

III

Inside an Amphitheatre	77
Before The Roman Remains	79
Mistral's Folly	80
The Rock Tombs Of Montmajour	81
Fallen Aqueduct	82
The Tower Of St Trophime	83
The Rock Necropolis	84
Crossing The Camargue	86
The Towers Of Castillon	87

Author's Notes   91

Acknowledgements

Some of these poems first appeared in the following publications, to whose editors I express my gratitude: *Agenda, Decision* (Germany), *Deus Ex Machina* (Holland), *Poetry Salzburg, Poetry Wales, The Shop* (Ireland), *The Warwick Review*, and *The Wolf.*

I should also like to thank the Stanza Poetry Festival in St. Andrews, the Ledbury Poetry Festival, Poetry Hearings (Berlin), Poetry on the Lake (Orta, Italy) and The Granada International Poetry Festival (Nicaragua) for inviting me to read in 2010–2011. I am also grateful for the support of Black Herald Press (Paris).

I

You must be ready to burn yourself in your own flame: How could you become new if you had not first become ashes?

— NIETZSCHE

Guided Tour Of The Ruins

Gather round, ladies and gentlemen,
and behold, for this was their city
their profound well, reflecting
a sad constellation of cheap tin stars.
Nourished on the hampers of decadence,
still they breathed in night's mint air
and under the elaborate tortures
of their own design, finally confessed . . .
Let us begin downtown, when,
on gala night, the hysterical movie star
was suddenly impaled
on a lance of white-hot realisation.
How she struggled to swab her wound
as the onyx limousine pulled away.
Let us remember, ladies and gentlemen,
the day when all finally awake
and fight to take cuttings
from madmen's brains.
Imagine, if you will, how worms feel
when finally the rotten apple gives.
Imagine the hardest winter,
imagine the longest scream
unable to fade, for that is how
this generation lived . . .

The Extinction Plan

Moments of pain, progress driven,
the unwelcome clarity of time's incision
enhanced by the new drug day,
where late crimes roll and bask
and suddenly woken eyes, lepers
peer in on hastening apocalypse.

The drone of no return, the settling
of old scores, of charcoal petals,
the cinder path of all that is predicted.
She who never arrived one step ahead
and all around you the embalmed
the catacombed, erect in their niches.

The extinction plan in motion,
as cut price flights steeply climb,
over Ensor's cornered skeleton.

In order to go on, Schubert pens,
Munch paints *Death and the Maiden*.
Strindberg runs through the Latin Quarter
brandishing his hands, black and burned
from experiments with sulphur.

Each repeats what has gone before.
The earth can take another sack of fear,
a single life's strict toiling,
embittered aging, the dead weight of loss,
a case of cherished photographs
and a few last sprigs of joy.

No one wants to be dust.
No one wants their love left out,
but nearly every wheel finds the rail
and follows the tramline to lust.

In one dive billions of krill find God.
Ghostly, like a low gas flame
they go on a while unseen, they exist
to explain the blue whale's darkness.

Christ On The Cross — Delacroix

Tearing away from the nails
towards the blind to come,
the twisted rope coil of flesh
and all of his will, the pale flame
licks up to the murmur of the crowd.

The eyes are driven up towards
the backward gazing retinue of gods,
eyes where hot coals have rolled
down the incline from believers' doubts.

Raised to Golgotha's prowling nimbus,
kneeling in thickets, a cliff, grim and hopeless
the light on its way but too far behind,
delayed at a bend in the river
where the watching face of the town
stoops instinctively to drink.

Human labour—two wedges hammered down
no Mary, no mourners, no soldiers
only bare brown blood-soiled ground
and the rent sail of a loin cloth
dragged out behind, the bloody ensign.

Above the broad bow of ribs
head hard back, taut, stiffened
like a strapped-down lunatic.
The lips, berry-blackened, alerted
by the awakening siren of putrefaction.

Hands pinioned yet still travelling,
nailed to prove they can't perform,
yet still this moonlit weapon is carried down
the tributaries of mankind, primed,
and perfectly aimed, a harpoon still shining,
still standing in the sea-sluiced wound
of death.

Nietzsche At The End

Yes, that's me in the armchair,
my face obediently lit by madness.
Dogs run with any bone I give up
and these silly old women fetch them back.
They lean in on me, fussing.
But I am still Dionysus
and with a terrifyingly thin hand
emerging from the blanket
I wave the world I gnawed white away.
What are my eyes now?
The shadow of moisture fading
too quickly from stone.
What is my heart?
A pebble in a black pool
on the side of the mountain
that never sees the sun.
Idiots!
And the stupidity that must come,
clockwork monkeys beating the skin drum
and my face seen again beneath the ice,
interrupting every thaw.

Sometimes This Genius Grows Dark

Feeding time in the fields.
Dark riders driving on horses,
flaming cypresses, windmills.
Somehow you must drain it all,
tear through the gauze.
All that's left a single eye that frames,
or this mouth rowing curses
over a lake of wine.
Dawn and a body slumped
in the coffee-threaded *pension*.
Over a torn brioche you thirst
for the forward dance,
those regiments and chorus lines,
chestnut, beech, sycamore, pine.
The copse calls out only for a moment
and you had to be there
fumbling with the cobalt, the chromium
exhausted by 'unquestioned potential',
the raised canes, the measured admiration.
The one and only arrangement,
a clear shot. Gone . . .
Nature slips behind a cloud.
Nothing remains but your seized prey face
seared by the comet's tail.
Later they gathered for the sonatas.
There you stood behind the player,
her fingers grazing into deep
un-reached black waters.
Insane craving to park your cracked lips
in the inconceivable shelter of her nape.

Now back into the Elysian fields
longing to step off, to strip, to shake trees.
But the sun is devouring your head,
the ruts chuckling at your patched boots.
Blood on the stubble, the rest barrelled
on the iron bed in the tiny room.
You count the canvases they brought,
these carapaces of hope.
They look like friends you once knew,
eight downcast angels bearing their shields.

Ice Warning

Now you feel the ice give.
Each rooted on his receding floe
and the last hard sellers of hope
slip with seals into dark water.
All are trapped together, even
the blooming girls thirsting
for their first assignments
and painted saints with visible halos
penned in by faded mortar lines, or
glacial lilies in the Sablon church
sustained by the last ember of their urn.
Wind sifts the chestnuts over a still canal.
From a velvet box they lift jewels
and hearts are turned to the past's
always emptying archive of light.
Later on a station concourse,
a homeless man begins to shout,
swings his life on a chain through fetid air
before the exhausted office girls
descending the iron clad steps,
who do not see and pass on
through the shrivelled leaves
whirling in eddies so furiously,
leaving no trace on the endlessly
swept stairwell.

Walser's Last Walk

In memory of Michael Hamburger

Seven slush footprints lead to
solitary death in the snow.
This is the body of the Swiss writer
they could not know.
That is his corpse, the storyteller,
a dark log causing a drift,
one hand snagged on the air's barbed wire,
sending a last futile command.
The grey felt hat sits expectant,
demands to be picked up and
brushed of snow by the formerly
careful owner.
Crystallised water made him
a pillow he never suspected.
Deliberately he dressed himself
for the possible pleasure of inertia.
Madness to lie there waiting
for the sudden snap
in the sprung coil of alarm.
Here they come with the sledge
right on time. Somehow
he made it over the line.
They raised his arms.
Victory . . .
But the race had moved on.
There were no flag wavers there.

Secret Of The Picpus Cemetery, Paris

Through a gap in the north wall
the tumbrels pass at night.
Lunges of torchlight trailing tar seize
the emerging forms of gatekeepers.
With invincible banality
the *gardien* checks his quota . . .

Wagons piled high with innocents—
priests, noblemen, ill-starred peasants,
sixteen Carmelite nuns from Compiégne
who, holding hands, advanced on the scaffold
singing hymns.

All rounded up on the committee's whim,
in a feast of bogus formality and derangement
of legalities delivered stillborn.
Two days later hauled from a cage for grooming.
Against their napes they feel the cool preamble,
the jailer barber's eager shears.

Now, two centuries on what remains lies here,
stacked in a lime-caked fosse,
wedged between the endlessly evolving
hospital buildings and elementary school,
whose pupils' playtime din draws
its strange undertow over the grave,
harrowing the vacancy, sowing new life
to tumble more beautifully into the abyss.

In the north wall the old lintel remains
and nearby a lone fang of palisade.
But the modern buildings sulk and bear down
as if to marginalise the charnel pit,
stifle the soul scraps penned in there
with the mercy pillow of concrete.

Yet the commemorative plaque endures
beneath the grey plumage of rain
and a few nuns still float gradually down,
dark leaves on a runnel between the planes.
Near mossy sepulchres you hear
the air's exhaustive account,
the slap of pouches on outstretched claws,
curses of the ever thirsty amidst
the cheerful clinking of spades.

The Lonely Ones

Sheep that strayed, suicides who, salted
turned away from the waves,
led hand in hand back inland
by the solemn piper strength.

Those who watched the angular shale
sigh free and somersault into the swell,
who saw each predator construct its kill,
saw through the slits in the dark crate
the fading cinder of an eye.

Horizon islands, peninsulas steering
the ghost boom of a ship in distress.
Eternally the cliff face collapses,
tricking the high hunter, training
the imperceptible tilt.

And you in the gorse holding the heaven
of a small child head that found you,
feeling the scalp, the hair, the breath pulse
calm to first snowfall on your fingers.

For warmth, all you grabbed from
the bullish days that came on,
but you watch it now from the shore,
your hoard, slipping away forever
through the sinking boat of bone.

Harrowing

Do you see the old moon waiting,
a tired gull tethered to the harrow
above the dawn reluctant field?

Do you see the rabid activists,
book brandishers, men of power
burning crude effigies for the crowd
and how even this evil is absorbed
by the eye blink of a deer in a glade?

Do you see the unblemished children
prodding the ditch with sticks?
They are finding out how it feels
to sink down an escalator in the mall
into the cutlasses of neon,
the vacancy encrusted men and women,
finery of the pit where coinage entrails
spill themselves unashamed.

Do you see this and weep for another age
which is only a mocking fantasy,
a tail pinned on the donkey,
a desperate raking of coals, brief glow,
piano played by the tramp's filthy nails,
or another rower whipped aboard
your heart's slow slave ship.

Feel the prow dip and drink,
only momentum and more funerals,
the warmth of a child and mother
slipping away into jaundiced snow.

The Clearing
In Memoriam Walter Benjamin

Gradually the dusk infiltrated
steering shadow onto baking rock.
The effect of the pills began to wear off.
Sprawled at the edge of a clearing, a man
one foot propped on a twisted root
sucking in the cooler air that now
worried heat's marauding butchers, the flies.
His will in spasm seen by every watcher,
prey thrashing in camouflaged wire
every fresh resolution tightening the noose.

Let them come.
Let them burst from the bushes now
and seize his futile human form,
his momentary hindrance in the plan,
the dirt count down in which
his berry-stained fingers dragged.
One on each side of Joseph K.
Kleist in his carriage hurrying away.
Cicadas gnawing at inexorable depths,
where death held to his bony chest
yet another comfortable hand.

The sun.
How had it found a way back?
His position, language had not strengthened.
Poetry could not be distinguished
in the gallows crowd that thronged now,
whooping up the mountain paths.
Owls solemnly lowered their ash capes.

He waved them away and recognised
his voice, a bell
that announced a leper in the valley.
Quite alone now and the only reply
the archive answers of silence.

Suddenly, hands reaching down,
the first interested scouts of the sun.
Stirring, heaving himself onto one side,
he drew the bent spectacles to his face,
a clinging worm magnified against his eye
hailing him through the glass.
Already warm and pungent the briefcase
sought its mule, the fully laden, the broken
impaled on history's phosphorescent shrapnel.
He sat up ablaze and shielding his gaze, rose
to formally greet his relieved companions.

Montaigne's Flight

Montaigne
slipped beneath
the raised cudgel of the plague,
abandoned his tower to owls
and the wind born cries of priests,
headed east, past beckoning cadavers.
He did not dare breathe,
but found air in others' words
he had carved behind him on beams,
words he potted like herbs, gaining
in the sun of his solitude.
They urged him back,
pressed him to fulfil his obligations
as mayor of Bordeaux,
but no light shone in the citadel
or in the black stump tower window,
until the day his horse and retinue
kicked up the highway dust
of ash and powdered bone
and in the depths of copses
the candles of the thirsting unborn
flickered to life one by one
to form a phalanx of gratitude.

Fatal Thrust

Lamb cries, their rough tongues
and all the hopeful gazing
through hot goose grass
the frisking, the jaunty muzzles,
new lives that will never know
the hawk's slyly opening blade
above the scrabbling thump of burrows,
the raven showing his young how
to slice through the sky's soft wood
and again over dark ringmaster rocks,
where the thigh blood of a beaten swimmer
is left as an Indian mark,
where Bear Rock's shadow squats
on the school group foundered,
horribly felt for,
bandaged alive by the tide.
But one scaled the shale
crouched and bleeding, determined
with bare hands to beat
on death's rising snout,
determined to baptize
the huddled forms with the moment
of safety longed for, to share out
the confectionary of a possible
coming dawn.

A man streaked with dirt
thrown forward by the explosion
of nature's strange psychosis,

pounds the salty door
of a still lit coastguard cottage.
The winch steel holds,
the last is fished out
hauled up like a monkey
felled by a dart.
How carefully they unhooked
the wind's ice barbs
and with guile they smoked
this near death out
only to preserved it, a foul
twitching brain pressed against
the remainder of their lives,
but safe from them
behind security glass.

Loss Of Habitat
One depression in a wider collapse . . .

Over the ancient cobbles of Damme
the low profile tyres thrum,
where once the lowly cartwheel
registered them one by one,
where the Dutch bike rattled through mist
and was leant against the peeling wall,
where canal, tower and windmill
were not drained by day tripper voices,
or the well-groomed middle classes
who step from Porsches and black Mercedes
to buy Buddhas and Mayan bedspreads.

Their barbarism is normalised.

In chic pastel-fronted bistros
guarded by skinny Mediterranean plants,
art gallery owners and executives
nibble ciabatta and goat's cheese tart.
This was once the Lock Keeper's house,
where the old man sat shivering
calling for more hot in his tin bath.
And everything old to be spick and span
each medieval brick repointed,
each crow step scrubbed and sandblasted
so the exhibit is deemed safe enough
and corresponds to the highest
suburban expectations.

Condolence Packet

Every face that still believed
noosed by the loophole of scriptures.
Those who sprung up the rungs of tombs,
or waded through the nettles of years. . .
Now they cannot run.
Now they cannot move.
Frozen in the cross hairs, we sleep
and only the giant ice wall breaks away
then crashes with unbearable power
into the sea.

Words of a spokesman – reassurance
The mass responds. Sand blows endlessly
over the fading stone lips of the Sphinx
and a lone voice none could hear
slips through the wires of dark rainfall.
A million planets found without life,
as on earth a couple just married
prepare to dance.

'Carnage 18' cleared to fire. . .
bodies obliterated, the rule of war
taped for future training purposes.
And a man in the desert, in the town
plucks his wife's singed hair from a branch,
pockets his child's glazed eye like a marble.
And a man in the town, in the desert
will now receive his condolence packet.

In A Lonely Place

Eternally the waters of the loch
encounter this uncanny inlet.
Perfected ripples purr in,
a few on either side of the herd
picked off by a fist of weed,
or a black rock's fin.
Relieved, the rest bear down,
only to swoon on bearded stone.
So calm yet unsettling this hazel cave,
moss farming a whisper,
dark water oiling the boulders
and with a twist and thrust
the magpie's dagger call.
Here the druids once stood.
Their white forms seemed from the loch
like candles in a sepulchre.
On our senses rest the remains
of their purpose,
why they stood each dawn
at the cavern's mouth in hope
that the waters might remember,
the breezes recognise a contour,
that they could turn and know
patient as a closing wolf,
the prey ahead had slowed.

Lenz

All I see through my visor
the pressing pall, diffused light
and crouched men setting snares.
The enemy . . .
I know they are coming over the hill.
But for now darkness has its back turned,
is still feeding, so I must stay quite still.
Otherwise it may come for me again
proving there's no dawn.

I must survive, take a journey . . .

Claw myself out onto the
unlikely shore of someone's eyes.
Let the last flare pick out
a child's hand in sleep, a star
lodged there before the vertical
downpour of partially rotted wars
and remorseless medal dragging
destructions.

Checkpoint

A last coin in the machine.
Then the hands of a deity descending,
forced back by the last glacier's
grey moraine, scree somehow contained
then collapsing, taking everything,
turning darker in the rain.
Crowd masks form to features of hate
beneath the violently pitching bier,
sweep their trophy to the shaft prepared
but a white horse stands in a field unaware,
tail broom flicking amongst wild grasses.

Brokers play on.
Believers work at their teeth with bone picks,
then clean their guns.
A body turns in bed, perhaps a lover.
Something is passionately said that has
strolled brazenly from lips before.
Somewhere the soil is turned, a will stops
then starts, and over dense black nests
the rooks wheel each evening
at the same moment as life falls away.

Sluiced mortuary, the registrar steps back
respectfully and the body is identified.
Blue flames wave through the darkness,
marshalling the obedient wood.
This is their calling, their dumb want
and the candle will burn right down
to the greasy stump. Only this is known.

The reliable scent of new mown grass
and living now, the small bird
grappling with a nut.

To tear others with teeth that took
all of evolution to sink into nothingness,
rivalries of the last reducing bergs,
and you staring down into the well,
finding only the sun's starved face.
Later, stars so sure over the lair of firs.
You wander in there and look up,
held at the moon's checkpoint.
Torchlight plays through silver birches,
at dawn a frozen warning eases
shots ring out . . .

I Am Charles Meryon

On waking, the first thing he does
is erect the barricades around his mind.
But those who took him tear them down
and leap in by lunchtime to loot all hope.
Everything is taken, even the sink
ripped from the skull wall
in which his reason was left to drain.
At night he stands guard with a sword
awaiting their return.
Baudelaire makes enquiries,
wants to meet, discuss the prospects
of an evil flowering frontispiece.
But as ever the etcher lets him down,
is *elsewhere*, cannot be found.
Now he's on his way to Charenton.
in a battered black coach
It's *dementia praecox*—
an acute delirium of the senses.
But over the terraces of the Tuileries
and the Place de la Concorde
armies of sea creatures gather,
chariots, tumbrels filled with excited figures
who ignoring the fatal diagnosis
to his rescue boldly race.

After Shingle Street

There are high performance hearts
that somehow carry the atrocities,
underlined by the writer whose body
had warned him, though he went on probing
and suddenly white-haired stood
knifed by the unconcerned external
in the courtyard of the fort.

And now they placed his glowing embers
in a Suffolk bookshop window,
where salty families pass unseeing,
mothers barking at bored boys
at tired toddlers having a tantrum,
fathers a few paces back trailing
the remnants of their proud aspirations
and grandparents teasing their shadow
from the next strata of children.

But he was not part of this.
He simply broke apart at Shingle Street
one November afternoon, a vessel in disarray
gave in at last to the sea's prising fingers,
the sky's mad hoarding of emptiness.
Watchers raced into the surf to save him
but it was no good, he was already deep inland
and the spilled treasure delayed them.

Chopin In Scotland
For Anne Beresford

Before they carried him upstairs to bed
he sat awhile in the drawing room,
his pale head a lone candle flame
groomed by drafts and the
perfected silence of servants.
They talked on, in French
so as to include their eminent guest.
He spoke in turn to please them
but it was no use, the soil gave way
and his hands lay felled on the sofa arms,
hands that slowly lifted,
hovered like hunger-weakened gulls
the coming storm denied a landing.
They had been so kind to him
and at first the vistas, the halls of armour
ancestral paraphernalia, had fuelled him.
But now, a month in,
he was an almost leafless branch
bending over the Broadwood.
Once more the hooves of sickness
had disturbed the pristine pool.
For long hours he fidgeted,
following the gardeners with their shears,
waiting for the topiary creatures to emerge.
Then, forehead against cool glass,
let go of the long dragged decision.
Return to Paris, a last month of classes,
his pupils' dresses darkening the passage,
until Delphine Potocka delivers her aria,

until the doctor's last conspiratorial whisper
and the life rafts of surrounding eyes
drift slowly away from his heart.

Horse Cure

Cut out quickly at birth
its vague purpose
destroyed before it knows,
the horse is harnessed
the horse is ancient, the horse is old.
Darkness grooms the absolute, the lens,
taking what light the blinker leaves
it revolves, rolls back on the brain
like a drained wave.

And the shouts of humans,
the sound of a can being kicked
over cobbles, roars, laughter,
leave the bowed head motionless,
a fruit life's worm worked through
fallen away.
Riders in bowlers on Bruges lanes
have forgotten it. Only a whip
on its flanks in their pudgy hands
makes them see it, but all fades so fast,
drunk by nimbus is the brief ray.

The horse responds to tourists,
those masks, held up again behind it.
The load is borne and delivered
past the main square, the *béguinage*
and back around the fountain,
whose drops the wind flings too late
over the parched hooves.

Then you saw the one who ran up
and flung out his arms to
embrace the noble head, one who
held the muzzle hard against his heart
and fired.

Hawkridge

At the first sign of opening the door
the wind wants you out of the car,
bundles you into the vast nets
of heather scent at Hawkridge
on Exmoor's edge.

Here a stream-stripped sheep's
bone whiteness shows ghostly
through wind river grasses.
You walk into the wilderness
and ponies cross the track ahead.

You run wildly through their eyes,
yearn to hang on to
their warm barrel backs.
But they move on towards combes
swept of the echoes of men.

In the first snowflakes,
the ewes have bedded down.
Carrying the sun's last strength
the red deer leaps from a ditch,
bracken trailing from his antlers,
weapon no-one expected
unsheathed by the concealed god.

Young Lions With Their Kill

Nature stalls, restarts . . .
Young lions crash into their kill.
Their splayed paws push back earth,
each an oak holding on in a storm.
Their muscled roars pin us to walls,
their jaws burrow out through ruffs
beneath the burden of blood-caked manes.
They swing them like chains,
rip the haunch of the zebra away
under a sick emperors gaze,
in a red haze of lonely destruction
they condone the pendulum pacing
of scavengers.

I Am The Reader

Look, I am famished.
Searching . . .
my eyes dip up and down,
then suddenly instructed
they pause, like the fox's paw
hovering in the limbo before
carrion scent commanded relief.
I search for what?
For information in order to illumine
the cavern where yesterday's bones
ghost a dark corner.
I'll wolf down those frauds,
executions and natural disasters,
energy-inducing slabs of crime,
even those quirky little tales
of personal endurance
and hail myself, after digestion,
a well informed person,
for I'll have a good grasp
of murder and extortion,
the eel-twisting of politicians,
the opulent misery of the forgotten.
The blood splashed on the mud hut wall
will dry out.
The sound of wailing around burnt shacks
will die out.

So tomorrow I'll be back, a spider edging out
to check for movement in the web.
I cannot help but read and imagine,
read and imagine, read and imagine

like the endless filling of a cistern.
It's how I measure the depth of the cavern.
My eyes lower pails daily
into the capricious inks of the void.
It's what they recommend I do,
if I wish to survive.

The Silence

Finally they have come to sew up
my occluded eye.
No resistance, no last stand
for I am paralysed.

Only the good eye, sensing Death
stand up from the Styx and smile,
frantically paces its socket,
forcing its bloodshot cornea to buy time
where the thread and needles ply.

A sack of spoiled grain, I slump
in the *tricoteuses*' laughter,
serving a sky that after decapitations
is cheerfully scrubbed with birdsong.
In twenty minutes the task is done.

I feel no pain.
I hear only the shriek of my remaining eye
alert to the monstrous responsibility,
ready to cover the lost one's dignity,
to bear the fallen load, to redeem
the soundless conspiracy of surgeons.

In Culbone
For Alyson Hallett

New lambs cocooned in crevices
silently watch you descend.
All the pennants are flying
on the wire and bitten hawthorn.
In the hill weave, the wave sound of cropping.
Steep is the path and lonely
to the neck of the enchanted wood,
the mossy funnel that pulls.
It is evening and only a stray chime
can be found here,
news of the last seabird's death
or the held breath of an unfolding fern.
Down, ever down, always sensing
the ranging inward antennae of the sea,
the covert blue experiment
the beautiful useless industry
of men falling away, too weak to grip
to find purchase, those of today
glimpsed between the seasons
or ancient lichened trees so still
amidst shoals of laughing bluebells,
as the humbled one comes
for a glimpse of the great eye in azure,
the cobalt crutch that moving up
takes the infirm body lying there
on the lush precipice and has the sun
pick it clean of all the filth
it endured day in day out, when
held by the blood rushing undertow
of all those terribly severed men
the new lambs secretly cried for.

In The Ancient Cemetery Of Ukkel

In the ancient cemetery of Ukkel,
a sign declares that since 1958
no corpse has been interred.
Driven to dig by cholera fatalities,
across the slope they sowed tombs wildly.
Terraces once swept by bracken brooms
are scattered with porcelain wreathes
and plaster Christs broken in pieces.
The enamel photos are faded
so that whoever these unfortunates were
they now resemble white-eyed devils,
spectres or oddly defiant lunatics.
Everywhere roots and brutish shrubs
haul up onerous sails of ivy
onto crosses like shattered masts
or embalm chapels where purple bramble
slips a noose over a last valiant cherub.
Living faces of long dead children peer out
pale and sweetened by rot, with
chipped epitaphs meant for eternity
'Bless our little Stefan. Always in our hearts.'
At the crossroad Calvary
a black iron spike still impales Christ's
beaten feet to the cross
and somewhere two skeletal hands
are waiting for the moment
to release the stilled dove.

The Fears Of Charles Baudelaire

Who's this wretch they fished out the Seine?
carted off to the morgue in a jolting barrow,
a steaming jungle-pig trussed to a pole.
That's the way I'll go,
or kicking the air hopelessly
like a fallen cuirassier's mud-held horse.
Or perhaps like poor Nerval, turning
on the laughter-spit from the whorehouse.
Or maybe a knife, bungled endeavour,
my blood seeping through the boards
to stain the rolling surf of the crowd.
Or even to go on, my cloak the broom
sweeping me down every spiral staircase
and out under the dripping ironwork
of days, to begin the game again
as the chortling potbellied players
suck on their pipes of clay
and with fat forefinger, move my counter
into the last black square.

Darkness On Darkness

Henner!
Last lost romantic painter,
he whom the critics hooked
and dragged behind them, whom
they rolled in the bloody sawdust
of their columns.
'Darkness on darkness,' they gloated,
'Henner sees only the stain, the hole . . .'
But they rose too soon, and
Henner carried on, left
his smudged smoking glades; deep pools
where the dumped bodies of last winter
strain to drain the last movements
of a murderer's hands.
Henner who left Countess Kessler,
daughter of Munch's art dealer,
the still fresh tar of her black bodice,
her face a candle's last confusion,
a swaying wand that grazes still
above the bleached coral.

Fate of the Juvenile Gull

Alone on the quay
his old man's gait giving him away,
mottled neck and head hauling
the rest because it must.

The youngster calls without respite
and the sea saves the pathetic coins.
Somewhere the eye of a shark swivels
and in the Merry Maidens stone circle
walkers slow, unsettled beneath
the sinister wingspan of shade.

Still no parent lands and, resigned,
he watches his own horror forced on,
watches for some deliverance
a last thought may grapple with.

Or he may just slip through,
find Zennor church and wing graze
the rough cow tongues of rock,
or hitch a pale winter sun and ride out
calling to the impossible vastness
for scale showers and blood.

Repeat Offenders

Here they come, in procession
holding aloft the reliquary remains
of the blindness that shaped them,
filling the contours of streets and squares,
running out from their communal nests
to secure the fallen crumbs
of strangers' deaths, anything
to sustain their sprawling empires.

Herd that hunts, genetically bidden
moving forward with raw certainty,
coasting on the highways
of each other's interred doubts.
In the effective angle of the gibbet
many of their terrible faces crowd.

At Calvary and the foot of scaffolds
their fingers flex and curl
tightening around shawls,
weighing the stone, the rotten fruit
or lifted past survival force a fist
through the thick forest canopy of cries,
to puncture the cheek of the dignified
or delirious condemned with a steel finger.

Herd that habitually runs the outsider
into the cold citadel of space,
then turns back to coalesce,
to erase the hero's imprint and erect
over every mercy seeker their gaudy stalls.

Herd no-one will bring down,
off whose tough bark the axe-heads
of bold individuals harmlessly glance.
Spreading out or shrinking to a point,
carefully they handle the evil or
at the arterial lust jet they circulate,
hawking postcards of lynchings.

Herd that bears down with a glance,
pins a target on the running heart
or rises with the killer wave, too late
the beaten swimmer feels behind him.

The Antwerp Mannequins

Schipperstraat in Antwerp is where
they pose the dolls, flog the meat.
The butchers are well prepared,
neon-fringed windows of human height,
the ideal shape for the cut on display.
On bar stools, the eastern and far-eastern
merchandise has been arranged,
skins of all races, all sizes and weights
preened, basted, groomed, buffed,
prancing or slumped, reading a book.
When active they wink, cock their head
and some earnestly beckon.
Languidly they dance or lustily churn
but today no-one is tucking in,
so this one leaps, raps on the glass
while this one tries another tack,
blowing a wire kiss from her palm.
Then a man steps out from the tide,
enters briskly and an incision is made.
But business is poor, by the underpass
the pimps shuffle their threats, spit hard.
Men pass, men who may have loved,
resolved to their silent theatre
of sly glance or self conscious gesture,
for they are only passing by chance,
always on their way somewhere else.
But all they want is meat, to gnaw the bone
to tear the haunch and fill
the emptying barn of their hearts,
where so many rats have run through,
you can see the grease mark.

Faces In An Orchestra
For Ingrid Soren

Now those who had ceased to play
lowered their instruments,
closed their eyes.
I watched them all drift off
the woman lead violinist first,
for when she played
her eyes were half-lit coal lumps
fallen away from a blazing grate,
her deep red lips someone,
who walked past a morgue unaware,
had kissed. Then the flautist,
following the bird passing through
the leaf movement of piano,
or a beauty bite that locked
drawing gasps from under the shroud.
Finally a percussionist, who just fell away,
bobbed like a balloon, trapped in the gantry
strangely instructed by shadows.
Then all suddenly returned
as applause fell from branch to branch,
snow exploding snow,
forcing silence to extract
its first struck note and reign.

Advance Of A Rain Storm

Last to leave the darkening Orangerie garden,
as over the enclosing screens of woods
the sun is overrun, hooded like a hostage
and left to suck in the sacking of cloud.
Coming up for air, weary doves
blunder into the dead space
where the scouts of the thunder crouch,
where the foliage is search stirred
by any possibilities for pain or rebirth,
in this atmosphere that closes the door
behind you and the discreet surveillance
of death.

Colossal nimbus, field grey armoured
heaving over tree tops, tightening crops
and the sun's last attempt
to slip through swiftly dealt with.
In rows, frantic, the dead seed heads
hold their holed cups out in vain.
Then it comes with its wrong idea of war
the rain, and some bathe, rooted there naked,
old trunks laughing, saplings bent, enquiring
as if the rain forces onto them
an already used existence.

The rain has invaded and so the earth
widens its maw, offering territory.
Yet soon the occupier moves on,
and the rooks' eyes blink off the beads
in the murmuring canopy.
Driven on now is the startled new, what rises
is earth odour to tether the remains
of the one time shrieking leafage.
You cannot use the word 'holy',
but the same word is gathering strength
wants to live, and unthinking
dives suddenly off the ledge
of my streaming upturned face.

II

Eternity's icy wave would devour man's golden image.
Against terrible reefs his purple frame is smashed.

— Trakl

Drawing In Ash

'And then the Reichsführer Himmler
moved closer to the pit, peered in
and as the execution commenced
had the misfortune of receiving
a splash of brain on his cheek.
He staggered back, turned pale,
was almost sick and at that moment
I was obliged to step forward
until his composure was regained,'
said Wolff, drawing in ash.

In Galicia, at the officers' dinner
the scrape of a chair pushed back
and a heavily perspiring medical orderly
sounds his sepulchral gong.
'Gentlemen, I have the painful duty
to inform you, I cannot go on.'

Ravine of firs, commotion in a copse
body of a lamb emptied, flung like a glove,
and the eagle's head turns to face us
combed red with the blood.
Climbers darkly frozen, all of us
pinned on the ice wall of history,
unable to go forward, unable to go back
but still signalling, still breathing
drawing in ash.

The Survivors

Solitaries, monks, their sighs
found in the plumage of birds,
their sometimes holy bones pounded
to provide the killers' hardcore.

Forever the wind tears at the fir forest.
Forever fearsome armed men carry aloft
the jolting bodies of the martyrs.

Unidentified remains are bagged.
At the end of the line the white eye rings
of the engine driver who obeyed the SS
abandoned in a soot blackened face.

Footfalls that break the concentration of ghosts,
fingers that search, that embark
for hieroglyphs on pyramids,
or nail marks in gas chamber ceilings
even the blind cannot interpret.

With each downward pitch
the figurehead is submerged
and the breeze of a passing knife
terrifies the open wound.

Late hearts that stand ajar,
their storehouses looted
leaving only remnants defoliated
by the present's recycled sand.

Proudly the people signed petitions,
tried to swim out to the raft of morals,
but the current was too strong
and only a sigh issued from the filament
of the future's blackened bulb.

Beneath songbirds they stumbled
in the cinder storm of language,
with mossy crucifix, winking crystals,
their idiot charms of bone,
the late children, hand in hand
making for no God's steady flame.

The Shriek

Crows grown sleeker strut
over rut held corpses.
Wild men run into the woods naked,
rejecting all but the pale hands
of overwhelmed nurses.

A last blackbird trills in the glade
as a naturalist poet soldier
reaches for his journal,
a grain in the natural order,
he records everything but
the long scream slowing through sand.

Laughter of the alive, waving of helmets,
weapon scientists in white tunics
and straining horse haunches,
as for eternity the guns roll back
towards bare chested shell loaders
and overrun by shrapnel swarm
one side of a stretcher collapses.

Partisans finally cornered,
elite parachutists dropped in a copse
and a woman hung for 'terrorist actions',
blouse torn, breasts patterned with frost,
fresh snow, a flail of ice beads
and the taut steel rope on which she turns
sheds every god so easily.

Spy Hole

The airtight door is firmly closed,
no way out or in but the spy hole
where the interchangeable eye blinks,
just large enough for the flexing iris
—the necessary aperture,
but the snake's fang also hammers there,
leaving on the lens its dew-beads of venom.
Wipe it away, you the same species,
wipe it away and hear more clearly
what the unremembered whisper
behind every newborn's plucky scream.

Always the future with grappling iron
climbing back over our stubborn
rose smothered walls, emerging
to ask why we took the easy climb,
why we went around, skirted
the unrelieved face of compacted bone,
why we still don't know who reached out
and drew with their arm's last strength
in the ocean of discarded clothes
I am.

The future asks 'who?'
How many are coming to build
on a meadow of bone meal and ash,
to walk, unaware, over the sea
of browning photographs?
Look into the spy hole,
step back and consider the mountain
against whose cleaver cheek

a trickle of trapped lambs show like stars.
I know we will not climb there,
will delay at the fork, are already
picking our way back down.

Away, always away from the spy hole,
swept by the seductive energy of voices,
devoured by the great broiling sun
of our single most precious and worthless life.
They who waited to meet us at the high pass
with the emblems they had hidden,
with their last tightly coiled seconds,
they kept our future breath as a charm
a jewel swallowed, or set forever
in the darkness of a folded palm.

Last Hours In The Flak Tower
For Alistair Noon

A lull and his powdered face appears
again in the observation slit.
Somewhere in the collapsed countenance
bloodshot eyes, peeling lips seek out
any existence possible on the parched surface.
Blue grey rings around the sockets
where again he places the chipped field glasses,
searches where the *Hitler Jugend* were hit.
Notes a roar of movement, veers in to see
snatch squad lifting deserter teen
to a shrapnel bitten lamp post.
Hugging with gusto the trussed legs,
drunken dog handlers from the SS
on an impulse murdering spree.

Convulsion and the final construction
of their hearts' black honeycomb.

In the basement, a few ashen nurses
pass gamely through derangement
plugging holes . . .
A madman enters with a spring flower,
then someone else who will die
leaking orders to await the reserves,
to hold. He fingers the cool clip.
Mortars closing, a furious giant hand
tearing up rubble, searching . . .
Shudder roars and the shell happy
stagger in on their stumps

through store rooms, passageways,
the lava of rats. Strangers
pleasure each other, raw with extinction.

On the third day in the holding pen
stale bread rained down on them.
Sucking their grey crusts, and
chained to the collapsed masonry
of mankind's colossal failure,
they drained east.

Closer

Men, working men, labourers
some stripped to the waist, stood,
hands on hips surveying recurrence,
dolls scattered on a new planet's surface.
Workers caught by the secret shutter,
workers frozen before the wall of fire
no new generation can smother.
Reaching down, they rudely drag
the generation of *Now* back,
drag them with bare hands
and specially adapted hooks.
But those who strode in afterwards
dare not look, recoil from the heat
to finish the meal of fully living,
all they had abandoned half-eaten
when interrupted by the shriek.
And, as one, now heave their mass clear
from the path down which proceed
the pain-contorted heralds of atrocity;
from any ancestor feeling for a hold,
or any incomer who reaches for
the dangling rope of a possible history.
And this is how the many move closer,
ever closer to the further away.

I see them approach then grow distant,
I see them run; men, women and children
slow to a standstill on the ash field,
scattering before them a lunatic's
chance construction of words.
And I see the breath-clouds of dignitaries

dutifully gathered in January drift out
over wreaths meticulously placed, steadied
by easily retracted black gloved hands.
And with bowed heads all stand silent
before the wire's undying song,
before the silhouette of the basalt one
who begged to live, and begged again
who forced the still moving body of a voice
through a mile deep of thorns
and was not heard.

The Clip
For Matthew Sweeney

Tonight they showed the clip,
it was a rare discovery.
Heydrich in colour sits in the sun,
perched on a stool, turning pages,
roll calls of death, perhaps
the Wannsee guest list
or his wife's purchases.
Then looking up, carelessly
sharing an unknown quip
with a figure out of shot.
Yes, there is Heydrich.
The sun could not discriminate
and found his temples familiar.
Sweat set off the cologne
and when his mouth opened,
air crept in, because it didn't know.

At his funeral,
they placed the two blonde daughters,
already cold urns filled with ash,
either side of Hitler.

History Lesson

At the *Museé Historial de la Grande Guerre*
the children have filled in their questionnaires.
Helmets, rifles, shells, uniforms . . .
all confectionary to the proto imagination.
But they bypassed the mad woman of St Marie à Py—
one of Otto Dix's collaterals,
who stepped beyond the lime rows and lived.
Saucer-eyed, she offers a dry teat
to her babe whose shattered head
blooms brain on the blast-swept doorstep.
It was also necessary they did not absorb
the skull socket show of feasting grubs,
the moon's circle drawn on the suicide
and screams pumped regularly
from the bellows of black hedgerows.
Or a mortally wounded man
hoisted on poles, bouncing away,
held back from the prepared shaft
only by time's caprice, or the straining weave
of a blood soaked grain sack.
And anointed with the blush of exit light
they missed the final caption;
the spiked helmet demon German
who brandishes one bloodied breast
of the woman trapped under his boot,
and to a throng of jeering acolytes shrills;
'So then lads—who's for the second?'

Dead Heading

Name and regiment, age,
sometimes the date of death
and nearly always a rose in bloom
levered open on the polite white
tombstone's rapier edge.
Indecently aligned, chained,
they stretch for miles, each alike
rose and stone locked together
on the sky-sluiced deck of
the great going down.
I walked through reading names,
herbs bounded in the breeze
and a few tiny ornamental trees
easily shouldered the emptiness.
Then he called, a lance corporal of
The Royal Fusiliers,
cut in half by a projectile
as he dragged Arnold the new pal
over the belly of a bloated horse,
and for this was awarded a rose
which now requires some attention.

If it was my own garden
I would pluck those dead heads
with a lazy tail fin twist of satisfaction.
Impossible to pass by, so I do it quickly,
like a confident thief, already away
with the husk in my fist,
letting it drop, watching it lie
to be fallen on directly
by the probing muzzle of rain,

that also tasted time-chewed rifle stocks,
cartridge shale, helmets held by rusty soil
and the fresh petal eddy of the rose,
that abruptly unburdened, draws again
on the shadow of the rifleman's heart,
an almost imperceptible archaeological
shading in the mud, sponge to absorb
the bottled sighs of earnest descendants
who journey here each year to duel
with derangement.

Note Scribbled To The Unsaved

I have followed your driftwood of rage
around the lip of continents,
and because I was born
I have followed your silence.

I have unearthed your last diary entries
from a laughing man's countenance.

I have accounted for every one snuffed out
on austere platforms or in damp barns,
every fresh heart placed, a futile swab
on the flaming temples of the sun.

I have followed an aircraft
with slumped pilot and flak-shredded wings
the rushing air eagerly pulls apart.

I have observed the leather corners
of suitcases showing through the snow,
un-recovered on a platform
lovingly filled with warm clothes.

I have timed my breathing to your
still rising forms, and I have placed
each of your names in cold churches
where no one comes.

I have seen the monument and
laid a flower at the tomb,
and I have stood by the concrete
slit where a candle burns for you.

I have watched your hope gutted like fish
and thrown on a pile,
but of that nothing can come now

only the wind through poplars
that heave against cloud

only fresh animals which, sensing,
move around

only the unknowing who
on their way to knowledge smiled

and dutifully delivered this note.

III

When at night a man like him, of our kind, comes
past the place where he sank, many a thought he'll give
to the site and the warning,
then in silence, more armed, walk on.

— Hölderlin

Inside an Amphitheatre

Caves, relentless uniformity of
long liberated cells slant-shadowed,
leading off concentric wheels of wall
beneath arches, where birds sent mad
by tearing flesh flutter into niches.
Soldiers, attendants running,
the crowd drumming their sandal soles,
as beasts ordinary and exotic
slumped in reeking straw,
are hauled out one by one
like noblemen in The Terror,
or the entire herd lashed through
into the maw of sprung muscle,
into the rain of beams off mail and sword,
bright plumes, brandished helmets,
wives in wine coloured robes and tunics
smooth palmed, lavender scented
ladies shrieking for the guts of elephants
to flop out on the blistering sand.
Above them plaited nets of gold and silver,
a canopy protecting meat from meat
haunch of boar, antelope's liver,
gladiator's arm, the still roped feet of slaves.
Aromatic fountains intended to soothe
the hot blood fug swilling in the arena.
In vast caverns beneath ground
men with stabbing swords and chains
resolutely perfect execution.
Trees torn up from nearby forests,
dragged here for hippo, panther, rhinoceros
freaks to be chased, forced on, netted.

Now two fighting lions wearily gnaw
at the gale of screams. Dragging spears
they collapse in the camouflaged pit.
To surging cheers, pulled out on hooks
and heaved through gore and sawdust slurry,
as, in a blast of trumpets
the crowd reels, almost satiated
then gasps in awe at the unexpected,
the release of a thousand white doves.

Before The Roman Remains

A massive marble bust eaten away,
pockmarked, gouged, as if a pact
between elements were brutally violated.
Then two faces, features torn off
in the slipstream of centuries.
Man and wife one presumes.
Their fat purse paid for my presence
two thousand years on.
Ad 76. They planned ahead.
The Alyscamps, close to the miracle saint
and a prince whose coffin floated down the Rhone.
Front rank for eternity at least.
Eternity, freshening them up each dawn.
They almost made it, but for the foraging seasons,
brigands who scooped out their jewels,
wolves who ran with their bones.
Defaced, hammered, stripped was their tomb
and even the names provided sustenance,
skinned in a century by sand and rain.
Only a faint outline, but their claw
still seizing, their hooks drifting
waiting for our hungry hearts
to nudge them.

Mistral's Folly

Yes, they had their black toad
under the bed
to absorb the devil's venom.
Yes, they had their lucky charm,
paw of beaver, toe of heron.
But it did not protect them.
Neither did the glass cased
grottoes with serenaded maidens,
little boats on sapphire enamel lakes,
foxed lace, silks and dummies
strapped into the melancholia
of those light weary mansion rooms.
In the visitors book, the blind
stroke their Braille
'An interesting collection . . .'
'I am an American, thank you
for showing me another world.'
But it's over and now
the Arlésienne in costume
prattles into her mobile phone.
Below, the pillars of the forum
reel like drunks, hold each other up,
weigh up silence or futile heroics
before the execution squad.
We have browsed the baggage
all our insane sprouting levelled.
What souvenirs! Brief scribbled notes
from those who were murdered,
which floated from the cattle wagons
into the hands of a shepherd
whose tongue had been severed.

The Rock Tombs Of Montmajour

Somehow with primitive tools
they scored the recalcitrant surface,
kneeling to let the sun yoke them,
on the silent shore of rock still there.
Like rude orphanage cradles they appear,
moulds for air churls that leap out boned
leaving only black water in a corner,
a scatter of cones . . .
So tiny the tenants then, adult children,
unprepared for crows that queued
to unpick their trussed forms,
beneath the sheer war tower
from whose lowest crevices thistles fire
and a lone poppy yet unfurled
calls out strangely in its sleep.
Monks passed here, their cowls taut
in the Camargue winds, laying siege
from plains whose bending reed deeps
harbour the faith ossuary of lost mariners.
Now you are standing there,
curiously explored by twelve centuries,
and here is your hand
touching the altar with the mason's mark,
terribly alerted by six metre thick walls
to the single leaf fall of existence.

Fallen Aqueduct

Bones stacked at the entrance to history's cave
so long untouched, and when they are now,
only by palms which then touch faces
that will die. Here somehow
the collapsed spine of an aqueduct,
from whose bitter joints
the plucky thyme still grows.

Silence and cypresses blacker than onyx,
occult stalagmites shoring up
the mass of faith broken down,
crumpled spider, master who controlled
now roped to the ground
by the silver web of an olive grove.

Someone whose voice went unheard
marooned on a rock
with sticky rosemary and rising bells
near the crow-stirred estuary,
watching the moon set out once more
to smuggle itself into loneliness.

The Tower Of St Trophime
For Marie Huot

At dawn crows emerge from holes
in the tower of St Trophime.
Weakly the structure stands
as if time had burrowed deep,
honeycombing the pulp of centuries.

With first light, crows impose their shrieks
on its sandy gut and on those who walk
the cloister roof terrace in sun hats,
so slowly, yachts in the dead calm,
bow to stern in the broiling heat.

Doves in a cage at the tower's base
fly repeatedly at the mesh.
Sent mad by enclosure, humiliated
by the swallow circus, crushed by
the shining loco wheels of the swifts.

Prisoners and liberated beneath a sky
readying to indigo deepen and sink
night's irresistible bait
on the waiting hooks of stars.

The Rock Necropolis

Once I heard someone say
'Every new human being born is a
fresh catastrophe for the world.'
I thought this strange until I saw how
man calmly snaps the neck of every
hatching lonely atmosphere.
In the rock hewn troglodyte chapel
high on a mount above the Rhone,
even there you witness a murder.
Was it for them the monks hauled stones
to the honeyed summit with vines?
So the sun skewered guide could hear
his own academic voice repeat
while gathering the feeders around.
Candles for his oxygen they burn.
Snuffed, they descend to the pits,
reducing like dying foliage.

Only then do shadows dare to tread,
hushed pilgrims over the rock tombs,
infant-sized where water, perfectly still,
completed, moulds to muffle the ravings
of eternal emptiness. Where
the rosemary settles its hairy toe
beside the black spoon of lagoon
and tired moss takes the place
of all the organs given up,
released at sunset for dissection
by the strong ebony beaks of ravens,
who ate their fill to the filtering chants
when it was lonely, when there was beauty.

Before the road, with one practised swing
felled the peaceful forests,
upsetting the bowls that some still held
to drink the dew collected, to drink
what gathered silently and patiently
in the broken skulls of monks.

Crossing The Camargue

Scalding plains that shelter death,
along whose edge mercury beads,
the molten cars, somehow pass.
Hedges of reed always agitated
and grit thrown by the unswerving
sower of the warm salt wind.
Solitary lagoon.
Design long melted, dream
of a white horse, hornless unicorn
on a tiny island standing so still.
The sickening roads lift and crack
and the thin frowns of shale beaches
greet unwelcoming choppy waters.
Famed, the flamingo fly-past,
unhinged spectacle, those stretched,
hopelessly assembled bodies
and too-pink skin, terrifying
like the sudden intrusion of a burn victim,
their bald vulture heads boring through
over the craning vehicle occupants,
dragging a maniac's unfinished puzzle
behind them, that somehow
in midair finds its solution.

The Towers Of Castillon

Three friends somehow overlooked,
not netted, slung into the *zone touristique*,
not manicured for mammon
like pinioned Les Baux,
but ruins in rude health
still loved by the emerging moon.

Alone now and perhaps also
when a legion passed,
welcoming dove or hawk,
Saracens emerge through thyme
and gentle melancholy leads the blind
donkey over the aromatic outcrops.

Let them live on, these three.
If chased down by the functionary
know they cannot run, or be coaxed
into some restorative collapse.
Don't 'see their potential'
or shame them with easy access.

Don't mention progress
near their tender rubble keeps.
Don't remind them they were breached.
Once was enough.
Let them fill with stars when we retreat
and their worn stump of steps
lead in what comes of our destruction.

It is a word, a rustling or knocking, that is endowed with the power to call us unexpectedly into the cool sepulchre of the past, from whose vault the present seems only to resound as an echo . . .

— BENJAMIN

Author's Notes

For the benefit of those who may be interested, I include notes on the background to some of the poems:

'Nietzsche At The End' (p.10)

Friedrich Nietzsche (1844-1900)
Mentally and physically debilitated, the great philosopher and poet spent the last years of his life in a nursing home in Weimar. During Nietzsche's final summer, Hans Olde took a series of remarkable photographs - deeply moving images which bear witness to the pathetic state Nietzsche had reached. But they also display certain preternatural qualities which elevate them from mere physical representation. The originals are displayed in the museum of the *Nietzsche House* in Sils Maria, Switzerland.

'Walser's Last Walk' (p.14)

Robert Walser (1878-1956)
A Swiss German writer whose novels and shorter prose works are invested with a precarious genius that defies coherent analysis. Walser's exceptional poetic sensibility and his largely impoverished itinerant lifestyle demanded a high price of his mental constitution. The last three decades of his life were spent in a mental institution at Herisau. He was found dead in a snowy field on Christmas day after embarking on a final walk. A photograph of his corpse taken shortly afterwards by the local police exudes an air of serenity rather than morbidity.

'Secret of The Picpus Cemetery, Paris' (p.15)

The little known Picpus cemetery in Paris is located in the eastern part of the city, in the barely visited 12th arrondissement, an area traditionally home to ecclesiastical buildings, religious schools and convents. It was the burial place of numerous victims of The Terror during the French Revolution, their corpses arriving daily by cart from the guillotine at nearby Place de la Nation.

The writer Stefan Zweig and poet Rainer Maria Rilke are two notable names whose sensibilities were informed by the romantic seclusion of the cemetery, which Rilke declared 'the most lyrical in all Paris.'

'The Clearing' (p.19)

Walter Benjamin (1892-1940)
Now much celebrated, the Jewish philosopher, essayist, translator and critic, Walter Benjamin, was a prominent name on the Gestapo's arrest list during the Nazi occupation of France. Escaping Paris in the nick of time, he headed south across the Pyrenees, planning to traverse Spain then embark from Portugal for the United States. The journey was arduous and Benjamin suffered from a cardiac condition. On the day before arriving at the border his companions descended to a village for the night, but the exhausted Benjamin determined to remain on the mountain and spent the night alone in a clearing. They reunited the next morning, reaching the Spanish border town of Port-Bou that day, only to find themselves trapped. New repatriation orders issued by the

Franco government meant they would be sent straight back to France and the waiting Gestapo.

Cornered, despairing and overwhelmed by the rigours of his flight, Benjamin took a fatal overdose of morphine, thereby evading his would-be executioners. However, the following day, local officials on whom this suicide had made an impression, relented and permitted the remainder of the party to pass on into Spain.

'Montaigne's Flight' (p.21)

Michel de Montaigne (1533-1592)
An influential writer of the French Renaissance, whose celebrated essays have been drawn on by virtually every literary intellectual figure of note since. Montaigne travelled at intervals from his chateau and its library, on whose very beams he had carved his own set of commandments, but always returned to the sanctuary of his citadel. On one occasion in 1578 he set out across Switzerland, Austria and Italy, in part to find a cure for the kidney stones which bedevilled him. In 1585 he was obliged to flee during an outbreak of plague.

'Condolence Packet' (p.25)

Name ascribed to the gift donated by the US military in Iraq to the bereaved relatives of victims lost to 'collateral damage'.

'Lenz' (p.27)

Writer and dramatist Georg Büchner's poetic prose fragment on an episode in the life of *Sturm und Drang* author Jacob Lenz (1751-1792), is a visionary tour de force housed in a biographical narrative. Büchner published his novella in 1835 and it is now widely regarded as precursor to the modern prose form. *Lenz* was translated into English decades ago by the poet Michael Hamburger and after years languishing in obscurity has recently reappeared in a welcome new edition.

'I Am Charles Meryon' (p.30)

Charles Meryon (1821-1868)
Son of an English physician, yet largely ignored today in the Anglophone world, Charles Meryon was a superior artist and one time sailor, who favoured the medium of etching. He sought to communicate the architectural soul of pre-Haussmann Paris through a series of remarkable works inclining towards the visionary and eventually the fantastical. They were also exemplary works of craftsmanship.

Diagnosed with 'an acute delirium of the senses', Meryon was admitted in 1858 to the notorious asylum at Charenton. Although after treatment he was later released, increasing melancholia and a growing persecution complex became overwhelming and he was re-admitted. Insane, he died there in February 1868.

'Darkness On Darkness' (p.44)

Jean Jacques Henner (1829-1905)
This Alsace born French painter's work was given a welcome airing at the *Musée de la Vie Romantique* in Paris (2009), and is on permanent display in the *Musée Jean Jacques Henner* in the 17th arrondissement of Paris. Henner's landscapes especially have a unique dreamy fuliginous quality which allows them to moor comfortably alongside the more overt symbolism of Moreau and Redon. Henner was a victim of critics who saw only a morbid proclivity for shadows, and failed to understand his attempts to find expression for the undisclosed in nature. Later however Henner was the recipient of awards and medals for his work and was accorded the respect his achievements deserved.

'Drawing In Ash' (p.57)

Karl Wolff was a high ranking member of the SS who became chief of staff to Himmler, meaning that in virtually every photograph taken of the Reichsführer SS, Wolff is seen by his side. Wolff was a key witness interviewed on the iconic *The World at War* television series (1973). There he recounted an episode when Himmler, keen to review the grisly handiwork of his executioners, succumbed to human revulsion and almost fainted.

'Last Hours In The Flak Tower' (p.63)

The immense flak towers which ringed Berlin during the Second World War were a German phenomenon. The German infatuation with concrete and bunkers began in the previous war, especially around Ypres, when having secured the high ground they constructed forts and colossal concrete edifices from whose surfaces the allied shells merely glanced off. In the following conflict concrete was again poured into the Atlantic Wall defences and the giant Flak Towers. The latter had a platform on top for the sky-ranging guns and a warren of dank tunnels and bunkers beneath for literally thousands of civilians to shelter during air raids. Most of these monsters were removed by the controlling powers during the rebuilding of Berlin, but the one at Gesundbrunnen in the district of Wedding mocked French demolition charges and is today a museum.

'The Clip' (p.67)

Unlike Himmler, his ruthlessly efficient deputy Reinhard Heydrich visibly represented the Nordic Aryan ideal. Among the atrocities the ruthless Heydrich committed as head of the Gestapo and Reich security services, was to organise the notorious Wannsee conference in January 1942. In a palatial lakeside villa rented by the SS, senior Nazis representing all offices of the German Reich met for two hours to formulate logistical plans for the extermination of the entire Jewish people in Europe.

In May 1939, Hitler had received Heydrich, Himmler and

Wolff at the Obersalzburg, an event recorded by rare colour footage, showing the genocidal godfathers relaxing in civilian clothes on the sunny terrace, looking more like a benign gathering of provincial schoolmasters.

'Mistral's Folly' (p.80)

Frédéric Mistral (1830-1914)
French writer who championed and wrote in the obscure Occitan language of old Provence and set out with considerable zeal to safeguard increasingly threatened traditions. Receiving the Nobel prize for literature in 1904, Mistral used the financial windfall to create a museum in Arles to house all manner of objects relating to this endangered culture. Known as the *Musée Arletan*, it is still open today and the exhibits are little changed from Mistral's time. However, the dereliction of its noble intent leaves an unsettling ambience from which the visitor eventually flees.

WILL STONE